Advanced Praise For:

MY LIFE AND WALK
WITH GOD

Tony has dedicated his life to serving God and has inspired everyone who knows him. Thanks, Tony, for pouring knowledge and wisdom into all the youth at the Mel Blount Youth Home as our choir director. He is a true servant of God and this book is evidence.

~Mel Blount, Former Pittsburgh Steeler,
Founder of Mel Blount Youth Home

My big brother Anthony told his life story, his musical journey, and his walk with the Lord with such fervor and integrity. Just to hear his story, his mountains and valleys and knowing he included me and my family is an honor.

All of my musical accomplishments lead straight to what Anthony poured into me as a child and now as a man. Well done my brother, the journey and your story is far from over.

~Paul Boutte,
Musician and Brother

Despite difficulties in life you'll realize that there is hope, regardless of what you thought was the ideal life. Pops' story is an example of God's love, protection, provision, and much more. After reading this book I pray you'll draw closer to God as you feel and see the manifestation of God's Word come alive in your life.

~Walt Francis,
Intercessor and Multimedia Specialist

What a life…what a journey…what a testimony of the love of Christ in the life and legacy of one Anthony "Pops" Mitchell.

If hope, inspiration, and a deeper level of faith is what you seek, this book is a must read because it is filled with adventure, joy, laughter, heartache, pain and ultimately triumph and victory in Jesus!

~Dwayne Fulton,
"The Maestro"

My Walk and Life with God is a must read. This book shares how to face adversity, keep the faith and emerge triumphant in Christ as long as you persevere through life's challenges.

~Rev. Karen Jones,
Friend

From a young age, the stories of our elders have always captivated and inspired me. Anthony "Pops" Mitchell's story is no different. I've been fortunate to know Pops as a mentor, teacher, colleague, and friend. He's not only a legend in our city, but also a giant in the music industry. You will find yourself deeply inspired and blessed by Pops and his incredible life journey.

~Trini Massie, CEO
T. Lopez Music

All I can say is wow! My friend Tony has dedicated his life to singing and playing for the Lord and I thought I knew all there is to know about him. This book will help you see the hand of God on Tony's life and how He brought him where he is today.

~Pastor Nathaniel Pennybaker,
Senior Pastor, Triedstone Baptist Church

This heartfelt memoir from my "Road Dog" Anthony Mitchell chronicles a life filled with love, unwavering faith, and the power of family. This is a testament to overcoming challenges with faith and perseverance, reminding us of the transformation and hope are always within reach when you let God lead.

~Valetta O'Kelly
Musician and Worship Leader

Pops as an elder is the definition of faith. His swag is attractive to younger men like me because he has walked the journey and he walks what he talks. This book will teach you how to be a Godly man.

Corry J. Sanders, Author
Lessons From the Chair

My "Poppa Bear" is a walking epistle. Once you start reading *My Life and Walk With God*, you will find yourself strolling alongside Pops as he takes you on his life's journey. You'll see the hand of God throughout this book.

~Latika Smith,
Spiritual Daughter

MY LIFE AND WALK WITH GOD

ANTHONY "POPS" MITCHELL

MY LIFE AND WALK WITH GOD

THE GIFT OF LETTING
GOD HAVE HIS WAY

My Life and Walk With God: The Gift of Letting God Have His Way
Copyright © 2024, by Anthony "Pops" Mitchell

ISBN: 979-8-9910453-1-5
Library of Congress Control Number: 2024914868

Published by: InSCRIBEd Inspiration, LLC.
Printed in the United States of America

Author Photos: Greg Tot
Internal Layout and Design: InSCRIBEd Inspiration, LLC.
Edited by: Janell Jones, PhD, Janese Jackson, Penda L. James
Cover Art: Studio Brooklyn Elite

DEDICATION

This book is dedicated to my mom, **Louise Fields** for all of the things that she has done to make me the man that I am today.

FOREWORD

Anthony "Pops" Mitchell is a literal living legend!

I can remember meeting him when entering the sanctuary of Mount Ararat Baptist Church in July of 1997. Hearing him minister through song during worship, I knew then, what I came to understand better later; he is a deeply committed man whose gift and passion are undeniable!

For 27 years, Pops has been a pillar in the ministry of Mount Ararat, an incredible encouragement, and a support to my pastorate.

You will find *My Life and Walk With God: The Gift of Letting God Have His Way* to be an inspiring and riveting story! The young and old alike find him to offer fascinating conversation and jovial engagement. He is a treasure.

History will no doubt record that "Pops" has blessed lives too numerous to count. I'm glad that I was privileged to do ministry in the season of his life.

Be Blessed,

Rev. Dr. William H. Curtis, Pastor
Mount Ararat Baptist Church
Pittsburgh, PA

ACKNOWLEDGEMENTS

I want to thank **God,** first. Thank you for the growth in me and the love You placed in my heart. I now understand why I had to go through it to get to it.

To my lovely wife **Bea**, thank you for loving me enough to put up with me all this time.

Gail, my loving daughter, thank you for being there through the hard times and for loving me and encouraging me. Thank you for reminding me that everything is going to be alright.

Mike and Janell Jones, PhD., thank you for the love you have for me. This book would not have been possible without what you did to help me get started.

To my Pastor, **Rev. Dr. William H. Curtis**, thank you for being an encourager with your anointed words. My life and walk with Christ are strengthened because of you.

Thank you to my helpers: **Trini Massie; Dwayne Fulton; Walt Francis; Diana Lowe; Rev. Karen Jones; and Penda L. James**, my Scribe Coach.

CONTENTS

For I the LORD thy God will hold thy right hand, saying unto thee, Fear not; I will help thee.

Isaiah 41:13

IF I LET GOD HAVE HIS WAY

I was blessed to have been born in Memphis, Tennessee on November 6, 1942. Through hurt, pain, and sickness, my mother, Louise Fields, had me when she was fifteen years old. She moved to Buffalo, New York to find work and a place for us to live. Mom had a sister, Aunt Mabel, who lived in Buffalo.

Although it was difficult for her, my mother moved up North and left me in the care of my grandmother, Lavada. Here is a picture of my grandmother.

Even though I did not have the privilege of living with my mother or father during my early years, I was very blessed by the love of my family. When family members would talk to me about my mother, I did wonder why I didn't live with her or why I did not know my father, but living close to a lot of family in Memphis made that burden easier to carry.

My grandmother and our extended family members were the type of people who liked to hug and kiss me all the time. I know that's why I have that trait today —being kind, loving, and caring is in my nature.

Under Their Wings

Besides my Aunt Mabel, My mother had other siblings: Aunt Teresa, Uncle James, and Uncle Alpheus. They both took me under their wings. Aunt Teresa lovingly cared for me as a child and as an adult. She and Uncle Alpheus would take me different places with them around town. Uncle Alpheus was a well-known minister of music in Memphis and he took me to his musical engagements at local churches and other functions where he played.

Mom had an uncle named Lawrence who took me fishing. My grandfather, Lloyd Fields, lived on a farm with his second wife Lela and their three daughters: Sallie May, Georgia, and Mazie Lee. On my maternal grandfather's farm I learned to pick cotton and vegetables and tend to the animals. I liked working with the horses, but I didn't know how to stay upright long enough to ride them. I didn't know how to control the horse with the bridle.

My Aunt Elmira, grandma's sister, came to get me when I was seven. She had told my mother, "I will take him to Chicago to live with me and your Uncle Edward, that way you don't have to come so far to get him." I stayed with them for three years and every time my mother would hint that she was ready to come get me, Aunt Elmira and Uncle Edward would say, "Let him stay another year." I was torn between them all and it was unreal to have so many loving people thinking about me.

Aunt Elmira used to joke with me, "I'm not going to let your mother have you." I was ten when my mother was finally able to come get me. Leaving my family in Memphis to go to Buffalo with my mother was bittersweet; I hated to leave them behind, but I was excited to be with my mother.

I think Aunt Elmira and Uncle Edward loved and missed me so much that they were inspired to have two biological children of their own after I left.

"Sometimes the wagon was heavy for me to lug around, but I made it happen . . ."

~Pops

MY LIFE AND WALK
WITH GOD

MOVING TO BUFFALO

When the day arrived I was so excited to see my mother! I sat next to my bags looking out of the window watching cars drive down the street. When she pulled up in her car, I said to myself, "Wow, that's my mom!" I was so happy.

After the car was packed and we were driving away, I felt strange. I had to get used to being somewhere new, and separated from the family I had grown so close to over the years. But I was with my mom, so none of those things mattered. I had longed for her and we were finally reunited.

Aunt Mabel couldn't wait to meet me the next day. When we met she kept saying, "This is my little nephew!" Aunt Mabel seemed so happy to have me in Buffalo, pinching my cheeks and squeezing me so tightly that I couldn't breathe. I felt welcomed by her warmth and I could tell that she loved me to death.

Mom and I lived in a small, one and a half bedroom apartment in a boarding house. I slept on a bunk bed and mom had her own bed. The landlord would sometimes cook for us. I think she enjoyed having a little boy around the house. She used to try to trick me into eating things that I never had before. One time she fixed eggs and pig brains. I thought it was good, but when she told me what it was I got sick.

Making the Adjustment

It took me a little time to get to know my mother, but I was glad to be living with her. She worked in a laundry factory and because we didn't have a lot much money she took a lot of overtime hours. In fact, my only two outfits were for school and church. I understood that my mother wanted to make sure I was comfortable living with her, but I hated that she was always tired. When she could, she would teach me how to cook, wash clothes, iron, and clean so I could help around the house.

Sometimes Mom took me to work with her. I liked when she would show me how to do her job. Mom patiently taught me everything she did at the laundry factory: how to wash sheets and pillowcases and how to press them. I was eager to learn anything I could because I wanted to make things easier for her. Watching my mother work so hard, I thought about ways that I could bring in additional income. It was important to me to help with some of the bills and other things we needed or wanted.

Fifth Grade

In 1952 I was in grammar school at Public School #31. To help Mom I began delivering groceries and other items for a wagon delivery service. I gave her the money I made. Sometimes the wagon was heavy for me to lug around, but I made it happen, no matter how many trips I had to take. I would get out of school, run home to check in with my mom, and work for a couple of hours at the grocery store. I was always making work and my school responsibilities a priority, which was important to both of us.

"Family and music were always important to me."

~Pops

MUSIC IS LIFE

Mom and I moved into a new neighborhood in 1954. Back in those days, gangs were rampant in New York. I was feeling a little nervous because I didn't know if I was going to run into trouble at the high school or in our neighborhood. All I could do to keep from worrying was to be my authentic self. I loved music and singing was my outlet. Ironically, music helped me get to know people in the new neighborhood.

I used to sing on street corners near my home. Sometimes I would set appointed times to meet up on the corner to sing with some of the guys. It was fun clowning around singing songs by Little Anthony and the Imperials and Frankie Lymon. I met Lonnie Smith, a lifelong friend turned brother because he loved to sing, too. He lived in the same neighborhood and we both started at East High School in 1954.

At school Lonnie and I sang so much that we ended up forming a group called "Teen Kings" like some of the people we admired in the music industry. In music class we used to jazz up popular songs with our vocals; I would play the trombone and Lonnie played the tuba. People gathered in the hallways to hear us sing and we developed quite a reputation for our talents as freshmen students. I balanced our part-time gigs with my school work and a part-time job at a car wash on the weekends. Lonnie and I continued to sing and play with our group in high school.

We added a couple of girls to the group and changed our name to "The Supremes." Much too often, our musicians failed to show up for engagements, so we both learned to play the piano to accompany each other. Even though money was tight, Mom found a way to buy me an electric piano.

Our group had engagements at parties, dances and other events. I loved when we would perform at the famous Dellwood Ballroom. People would be dancing, having fun, and singing along with us and that was a wonderful feeling for me.

Music and Family

Around my third year of high school I met a nice young lady who went to an all-girls school. She and her friends came around one day when Lonnie and I were singing in the neighborhood after school. Yvonne and I became good friends and she introduced me to her parents. Her mom liked to hear me sing when we would come around the house.

One day Yvonne's parents asked me to keep an eye on her and her older sister when they were working late. We dated for a while and Yvonne got pregnant with our first child in 1960. Although her parents were disappointed, they liked me and knew that I was a good guy.

Because I wanted to take care of Yvonne and our baby, I dropped out of high school and went to an Army recruiter. When I told Yvonne my plan to join the military, she did not want me to enlist so I changed my mind. Thankfully I hadn't finished my enlistment paperwork. Lonnie and most of my friends graduated from high school and I had a job playing the piano to take care of my family.

A few months after my oldest daughter, Gail was born, Yvonne and I had a small wedding ceremony for family and friends. I thank God for our two beautiful daughters, Gail and Dawn. Dawn who was born in 1962.

Meeting My Father

My paternal grandmother, Mattie Mitchell reached out to my mother's mother for my phone number. I didn't know that my father's side of the family was looking for me, nor did I know that Grandma gave my phone number to someone I didn't know.

One day out of the blue in 1971 I received a phone call from an older woman. When I answered the phone she sounded so happy to talk to me. The woman said, "You're my Grandson. I've been trying to find you, boy." At first I thought it was my mother's mother calling so I said, "Grandma?"

She said, "Yeah, I'm your grandma on your daddy's side." I was shocked at her excitement, but I listened to her talk, "I've been trying to find you, and your daddy wants to see you."

I was stumped for words. I was thinking, "I am married with two kids, and here come my daddy. What do I need a father for now?"

I went to Memphis to meet my grandmother. If it had not been for the grace of God and changing my life, I probably would not have made the trip. I was curious, yet nervous as I sat in her living room and we talked. She had told my father that I was coming and was he hoping to see me, too.

This is a picture of me with my Grandma and my mother.

After my Grandma and I talked for a while, she called my dad and said, "Bubba, your son is here. You can come over." I had the same nervous feeling meeting my father that I had the first time I met my mother. I sat in my Grandma's house and watched for his car out of the window. When my father finally arrived, I couldn't wait to hear what he had to say to me.

I Am Bubba's Son

When William Mitchell walked into the house, my daddy looked so cool. For an old guy he had a youthful appearance and was dressed nicely. I guess that's where I got my style from. We hugged, and at first it felt strange to be in my father's arms. Hugging him, I began to thank God that I had a father who really cared about me, even though I didn't know he existed for many years.

The three of us sat down and in between Grandma's exclamations of "My grandbaby!" and joyful tears we started talking. I found out that everything that I thought about my father was not true. Growing up I thought he had abandoned me, but he did not know that I existed. He did mention that people had told him he had another son, but he didn't know what to believe because my mother never confirmed it.

As a child I had always wondered why I didn't have a father to take me places or do things with me. When we met, I could see the joy on my father's face. Over the years he did what he could to make up for lost time by calling and spending quality time. I was disappointed that my father was not in my life as a child and young adult. I was often mad, hurt, and did not care if I ever saw him. What I did not know was that my father's absence was not his fault.

When I met my siblings we started to have family reunions and get to know one another. My brother, Carl, who thought he was the oldest, asked, "Where were you when I was in school? I needed you to beat up some people." I thought that was funny. I had a total of nine paternal siblings: Carol, Howard and Marsha have passed away. Harold is a pastor in California, William is a deacon, Carl is retired, Rose is the oldest sister and Krissy is the baby.

This picture was taken in 2022 at my father's 96th birthday celebration.

The Completed Puzzle

I thank God that He used my grandmother to restore the joy in my life. Her efforts to reunite the family gave me a missing piece of the puzzle and took away the bitterness I experienced from not knowing my father. God showed up and showed out in our relationship and I am so grateful. Grandma got us together and she passed away in 1973.

The development of my relationship with my earthly father, Bubba, is a testimony to what I believe: that when you think it is all over, God has the final say. The love I received throughout my life from my family is what the world needs more of today.

"My walk with Christ wasn't that great back then and I didn't lean on Him like I should have."

~Pops

GOING IN DIFFERENT DIRECTIONS

Unfortunately, Yvonne and I ended our marriage after 10 years. I grew a lot from my first marriage. We had a lot to learn about being a married couple and what it took for us to stay together. We were both very young and didn't have the tools to make it work. I didn't understand the scripture, "What God has put together, let no man put asunder (Matthew 19:6)."

I now know as an older man, that sometimes what God has for me can be different than the path I may choose. I thank Him for His permissive will and for His grace during that time in my life. There were many blessings that came from my marriage.

Healing

I had a pretty rough time after the divorce. My walk with Christ wasn't that great back then and I didn't lean on Him like I should have. Instead, I was mad at everything and everybody because I just did not understand His will for my life. I stayed occupied by traveling with my band whenever I could. That kept my mind off of the pain I was carrying.

About a year after my divorce, I got into another relationship and my son, Marcus was born. As I stated before, my family is, and has always been important to me. I was close to and involved in my children's lives, keeping them as my number one priority.

A Transition

A local radio host and disc jockey heard our group sing at the Dellwood and approached us one day. He said, "Man, I got a studio up in Utica, New York. Your group needs to cut a record." We were all thrilled for the opportunity. In 1961 we went to the studio to cut our first record, "Baby, I Need Your Good Lovin." It did pretty well when it was released.

Lonnie and I had a connection with Jimmy Sibley, a booking agent who heard us playing in Cleveland, Ohio. Jimmy offered to give us each an organ if we learned how to play. We both took on the challenge and learned to play.

I exaggerated my age so I could get into Gleason's Club to practice every day. At first, I drove people crazy!! They would say, "Oh, that boy is up there again. Can you please get him off that organ?" I refused to give up on learning and so did Lonnie. He worked so hard that he made a career out of playing the organ and other instruments.

Around 1966 Lonnie started to play music with George Benson and a number of other notable jazz artists. After a major record deal, he changed his name to "Dr. Lonnie Smith," adopting the title because of his hard work, knowledge, and expertise. Lonnie was a teacher and a sought out musician until his death in 2021.

After I learned to play with confidence, Jimmy began booking engagements for my band which I named, "Little Anthony and the Soul Detergents." We traveled all over the country, even in bad weather. Lonnie was traveling internationally, we made sure to keep in touch.

"The voice sounded like it should have been coming from a big, healthy woman, but I saw a tiny little thing."

~Pops

LITTLE LADY WITH A BIG VOICE

"Little Anthony and the Soul Detergents" was traveling a lot for gigs throughout Ohio and Pennsylvania. We were called "the clean-up kids" because people liked our music and they traveled in droves to see us perform.

One day in 1962 while we were performing in Akron, Ohio, I walked up the street during our intermission. I walked toward a jazz club and heard a big voice coming from inside. The voice sounded like it should have been coming from a big, healthy woman. I walked in to see who was singing and I was surprised when I saw a tiny little thing behind the microphone. I stood there mesmerized by the woman singing and her big voice.

When they announced her name I repeated it to myself, "Bea. Wow!"

It was hard for me to leave, but I had to finish my own set. As soon as we finished I hurried right back to the jazz club and found Bea. I said to her , "I have a band called Little Anthony and the Detergents and I would like for you to sing with us."

She smiled and said, "I have a commitment with another band. When I get back I will sing with you." I waited a whole year for Bea. I couldn't wait to get back to Akron to find her. A year later I went to the jazz club and she was there. As soon as I saw her I asked, "Are you ready to sing with us?"

"Yup," she smiled. The day she joined our band we changed our name to "Little Anthony and the Soul Detergents featuring Little Bea." I felt so grateful for the new addition to the band. I knew something big was going to happen for us.

For our first show as a new group, we went to Canton, Ohio. The crowd loved us, especially because Bea is from Massillon and it was like being home for her. Her whole family came out to support us that night.

Close Friends

During our travels Bea and I became like brother and sister. We had both left our children in the care of family to focus on our singing careers. And we would often have heart to heart conversations, consoling and supporting one another. Traveling became our job and we were together more than we were apart.

After some time Bea became involved with the band's drummer. In 1968 they had a son together and named him Nate. Bea and her partner did not stay together long, but they remained cordial and co-parented Nate. Bea's partner left the group to go play with James Brown. We were happy for him to get that job.

I was tired of messing around with different women and I knew Bea was a good woman. As time went on we started to get close and were drawn to one another. Eventually we fell in love, and in 1971 decided to date each other exclusively.

By 1972, Bea and I purchased a house in Massillon. We needed a place to stay and recuperate when got off the road. We were thankful for Bea's brother and his wife who were keeping Nate, and we wanted to have a place he could call his own.

Marrying My Best Friend

One day in 1974, while riding down the highway, I said to Bea, "Let's get married." We decided to get married and I said, "We better get married now, we might change our mind." Within 24 hours, we drove to West Virginia, got married at the Justice of the Peace and went immediately back to work. Bea and I have been together since.

A year or so after Bea and I married, the band and I met James Lawson. We were performing at the hotel he owned in Harrisburg, Pennsylvania. James liked our act and he became our manager. He went on to book engagements for us throughout Canada, Ohio, West Virginia, and Pennsylvania. We traveled to various cities that included Montreal, Cleveland, Detroit, Atlantic City, and Rochester. We performed at well-known venues such as Birdie's Nightclub and the Crawford Grill in Pittsburgh; the Hollywood Club in Clairton; the Pine Grill and the Revelot in Buffalo.

In 1967 I wrote a song about a man and a woman's connection called "Will You Be Ready." A Motown producer heard the song while we were performing in Detroit and was quite interested in having us record it in the studio. He liked the song but he said, "The band needs a name change. Give it a name that people will remember."

Clowning around, I said, "How about "Samson and Delilah?" Everybody liked my suggestion for the name and the rest is history.

Samson and Delilah

Samson and Delilah cut our song, "Will You Be Ready" and it soared in the Top Ten on the charts above recordings by stars like Aretha Franklin and Sam and Dave. Unfortunately, one record company felt we sounded too much like Sam and Dave, and bought us off the air. During that time it was called payola debt. After we got off the air, Sam and Dave came out with their record, "Soul Man" which topped the charts and made history.

The band traveled through rain, snow, and freezing cold. Our travels were always strong reminders of God's work and presence. One day, while driving down the highway in our green, black, and gold hearse with white wall "gangster" tires, our driver fell asleep at the wheel. We went off the road and ended up on the median strip. God kept His hand on us, no one was injured.

Another time, while traveling to an engagement in Erie, Pennsylvania, I was driving the van with a trailer hitched to it. We hit an ice/snow patch and the van went out of control. When we started to slide, I hit the brakes and called out the name "Jesus!" Our path miraculously straightened up and I regained control of the vehicle. We knew that God had truly blessed us as it was only Him that could have kept us safe in that situation. Everybody in the van had a private moment of worship. All I could hear people saying was, "Thank you Lord."

While we were performing in Detroit, Stevie Wonder heard our song "Will You Be Ready." He especially loved Bea's voice and wanted to help us produce the song. Unfortunately, due to contractual arrangements with another management company, that couldn't happen. Stevie became a good friend of ours and sometimes he played with us when we were in Detroit and Rochester.

I met and was "adopted" by the Boutte family during the course of my travels in Rochester, New York. They used to come hear us play and Paul, my "adopted brother," was always on my coattails wanting me to teach him to play the organ. I taught him one song and he went on to learn to play everything and become an accomplished organ player. Paul is now a minister of music.

Samson and Delilah went on to get record deals with Poladora Records and ABC Records and continued playing with prominent artists, like the Temptations, the O'Jay's, Gladys Knight and the Pips, the Isley Brothers, and Dionne Warwick. During this time we traveled all around the United States and Canada.

We added more instruments to fill out our band so that we could have a much richer sound. We changed our name to "Samson and Delilah and Lady Godiva" then to "Samson and Delilah featuring Soulful Ron," and then to "Samson and Delilah and the Sexy Tiaras." We had a good friend named Eltisa who wanted to sing so we named her Lady Godiva.

"Their joy and appreciation of the music touched our hearts."

~Pops

GOING INTERNATIONAL

Little Anthony and the Soul Detergents used to open for the O'Jay's, a popular musical group. We became friends and we stayed connected as my group changed over the years.

In 1979, during one of our performances in Canton, Ohio, their manager approached us and asked, "Would you be willing to fill in for the O'Jay's at an engagement in Liberia?" They were overbooked and could not go. All of us were so excited. I asked, "When do we have to go?" It wasn't even a question; we were going international! It made me feel great that my friends thought enough of me and my band to ask us to represent them in Africa and stay in Monrovia for a whole week!

Changes For the Trip

I went to Memphis, Tennessee to get my birth certificate to apply for a passport and there wasn't one so they sent me to the capitol in Nashville. I located my birth certificate and discovered that I did not have a last name. That was a weird feeling, how did I go so long without a last name?

Up to that point, I had been going by "Mitchell," my father's last name. That made me wonder how I was going to get a passport. The staff members told me to update my birth certificate to include my mother's last name, Fields and father's last name, Mitchell. It didn't take long to complete the paperwork once I got everything sorted out, I was happy when I was able to get my passport.

Going To Africa

The band had to prepare to get ready for our trip. We didn't have to have a lot of rehearsals because we knew our set list, but we had to get multiple shots. The airline wouldn't allow us to take all of our equipment so we made a list to downscale. Picking out my wardrobe was my favorite part of planning for the trip. I went shopping because it was important to me that I look nice.

We prayed amongst ourselves that God would be in the midst of us and keep us safe. Bea and the band left a day ahead of me because of the delay with my birth certificate. I was concerned about Bea leaving without me, but I hugged and kissed her before she left and said, "I will see you tomorrow." I hated to see her go without me.

I was so excited to get on the plane and the flight took 17 hours. The plane stopped in Paris, France, for a layover and then we switched planes to continue to Sierra Leone. After landing, as I tried to pick up my bags from under the plane, Porters eager to get tips, were grabbing at them so much that my bags were damaged. I was upset at first, but once I learned that poverty was a serious issue in the country, I didn't feel so bad since my clothes weren't messed up.

I caught a cab to a boat dock and took a ride to the city of Monrovia in Liberia. I was met at the dock by the promoter's team. We got into a taxi and rode to the hotel. I was so happy to see Bea at the curb waiting on me. When the cab pulled up, my wife noticed a big, hairy black widow spider at my feet. I hadn't even noticed that I was riding with it the whole time.

Bea shouted, "Anthony, look!" The spider was trying to crawl out of the car with me. That was one of the scariest moments of my life! I got out of that cab as fast as I could! The promoters were all laughing at me as I jumped out of the cab. Through her chuckles Bea said, "You sure can move, can't you?"

I screamed and jumped back, "That thang would have bit me." I was jumping all around trying to make sure it didn't jump on me.

Bea just laughed and she said, "Don't forget, you are in Africa."

To add insult to injury, as we were walking to our room, Bea said, "Our room had some big, flying roaches. I already talked to the front desk about it." The hotel staff told her that roaches were a problem in the country. "They make Americans feel uncomfortable," the front desk attendant told her. "Most people often keep lizards in their home to eat them."

The hotel was clean, and it was upscale, but for us, roaches in our room were not a welcome sight. I said, "How we gonna be in the room with a bunch of roaches in here?"

Bea reassured me, "They told me to keep the air conditioner on to keep them away." Our room was so cold the whole week, but I didn't mind because I didn't want to see any roaches.

Sightseeing

The next day Bea and I were excited to get out and see the city of Monrovia. I had my instant camera with me and as we walked, I took pictures. People would crowd around me and ask me to photograph them. I did that for a while, and I gave them the photos. It made me happy to see them smile.
Bea ran into some friends she had met while there and I ventured off to look at the capitol building. As soon

as I took out my camera to capture some images, I was stopped by a guard at the capitol.

He said, "Who told you to take pictures?" His accent was so thick that I didn't really understand what he was saying. He kept repeating himself. I tried to explain that I was a tourist taking pictures and he said, "No, you no take pictures." He grabbed me by the arm and said, "You come with me."

At that time, a woman from the American Embassy interceded on my behalf to prevent me from being arrested. She told me that I wasn't allowed to take pictures anywhere in the country, unless I had specific permission from the capital due to the ongoing war. I was scared at that point, so I put my camera away.

Not even a block away from the capitol with all of its splendor and beauty, there was poverty. We saw the impact of Monrovia's ongoing war with people struggling to get money for necessities. There was overcrowding and squalor. Families were living in, and under shacks. It was heartbreaking to hear that some parents trained their children to rob other people's homes.

I was reminded of how blessed I was to be living in America as we witnessed the struggles of Monrovia's people. We saw piles of clothes on the ground that had been shipped into the country from second-hand stores. People were gathered around picking out items that they needed for themselves.

Sometimes at night I would stand on our balcony to look out at the city. One night I heard so much chaos as if it were the heart cries of people in the street. I then saw police disciplining children for stealing and they gathered them up to arrest them. It was hard for me to watch them going to jail for just trying to survive. During that time, shootings occurred on nearby beaches.

I didn't like the food much in Monrovia, not even popular, fast food restaurants. One day I had spaghetti with green sauce and something else that looked like spinach, but it wasn't. A guy in my group and I used to try to eat the hottest peppers. They put peppers in front of us and told us how hot they were. They tried to warn him not to eat them, but he played tough, "I can take it." He took a bite and the next thing I knew; he started running. They tried to give him milk to soothe the burning of his tongue, but nothing worked.

The only thing I did like was a swordfish meal that was cooked for us by one of the people we met. We were invited to their house and she grilled the fish outside. Bea is allergic to fish; I ate my portion of the fish and hers.

The country had one or two television stations, and I liked to wind down with a few shows, but there was really nothing to watch. However, I couldn't call home to check on my children like I wanted to because the connections were bad. After a few days, I was ready to get back home to America.

The Festival

We played in a famous musical hall and our performance was a hit! The audience, which numbered in the thousands, sang and danced. We played Samson and Delilah arrangements and songs by the O'Jay's. The crowd loved when we sang, "Love Train," the atmosphere was electrifying. Everybody in the room seemed happy. When we finished playing they did not seem to want us to leave, they repeatedly called us back on stage for encores. Their joy and appreciation of the music touched our hearts.

About a week after we returned home, the country's president was assassinated.

.

*"I couldn't fathom
what was happening."*

~Pops

HEARTACHE & TRAGEDY

Performing in Africa was a nice experience. I had enjoyed learning about things happening in the world, but I was thankful to be home with my family. Seeing how families were broken up and sleeping in alleys, I was glad that God had blessed me with safe travels. Seeing the hard times that people went through made me appreciate being an American.

As soon as we got off the plane we took the two and a half hour ride back home to Massillon. We didn't take much of a break; we spent time as a family, loving on our children, then got back on the road, after a few days. Most of the time we were working in and around Pittsburgh, Pennsylvania and Newark, New Jersey.

While we were doing a gig in Newark, I got a phone call that changed my life. I was getting dressed for our show when the hotel phone rang. It was Yvonne and I could tell she was upset. I asked her to tell me what was going on and she said through tears, "Dawnie has been diagnosed with cancer. She has leukemia." My daughter was an aspiring writer and she was learning to play the piano. I couldn't fathom what was happening.

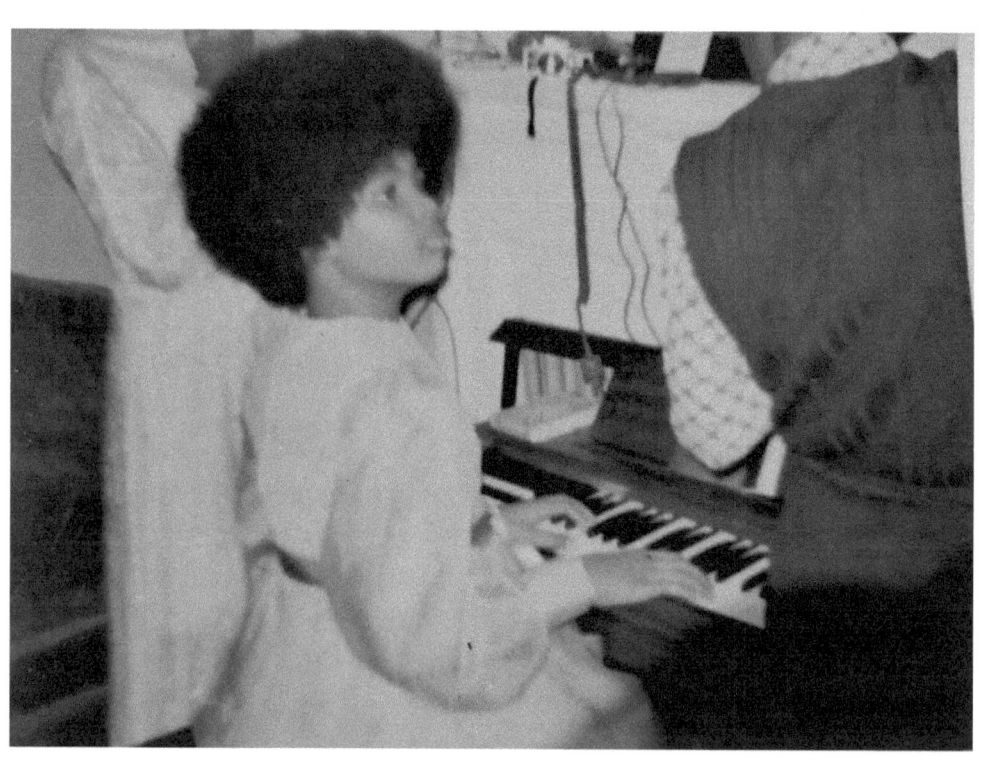

Processing The Diagnosis

I began to cry and I tried to find answers that I couldn't find. "How could my seven year old daughter get cancer?" Bea was out of the room at the time, but when she came back, I told her and she couldn't believe it either. She said, "Oh, my goodness, that didn't happen, did it?" Both of us were in shock. Even though I didn't want to go to work that night, I did, but even the music didn't soothe my heart.

We finished the gig and Bea went back to Massillon. I flew to my baby in Buffalo. I ran into the house, grabbed Dawn and hugged her close. I broke down in tears holding her. She wanted to know, "Daddy why are you crying so much?" I couldn't answer her.

Dawn's illness kept me running back and forth between Buffalo and music engagements. I wanted to be with her as much as possible, and every time the phone rang, I dreaded someone saying, "She's not doing well, come back." It was agonizing to see Dawn so weak and in so much pain. It was difficult to see her going in and out of the hospital so much.

There were times when Dawn seemed to get better, the doctors would tell us that she was reacting well to the medication, but then she would get worse. One night I was playing in Rochester, New York which was 70 miles away. They called to tell me that I needed to get to Buffalo because she might not make it through the night.

I left Rochester driving about 80 miles an hour to get to her. The information I had was that she was turning green and time was drawing near. When I walked in her room, her vital signs returned to normal. It was almost as if she needed to see her Daddy, and I knew I needed to see my baby. Dawn was fine for a while after that day.

About a year later, I got another call that she wasn't doing well. My former wife said, "You need to get here." I left a gig in Pittsburgh and flew to Buffalo. All I could think was, "Why me, why is this happening to me?" I arrived at the hospital and was sitting on her bed, when Dawn's blood pressure began dropping.

The nurse said, "I think you should call her mother." I was in denial so I kept putting it off. I said, "I think she will be alight." I held my baby and fed her ice crystals.

My baby looked at me and said, "Hold me, Daddy." I pulled Dawn into my arms and held her. She said, "Not too tight, Daddy. Not too tight." I relaxed my arms, and held her close without squeezing too much.

After a few minutes, the nurse convinced me to call Yvonne. When she and Gail arrived, Dawn took her last breath with all of us by her bedside. At first I thought she had gone to sleep, but the nurse let us know that she had passed. My precious, 11 year-old daughter died in my arms and I was devastated.

I did not allow myself to cry because I wanted to be strong for my former wife and my older daughter. I tried to maintain my composure, but at times it overtook me and I would leave the room and cry in a corner where no one could see me. It was a tough time for all of us. Thank God for my mother and Aunt Teresa who came to the hospital to comfort us.

Losing Dawn was the most difficult time in my life, particularly because I was at an early point in my walk with Christ. My mother and Aunt Teresa tried to help me keep my eyes on God. I remember one of them saying, "God will make a way." I didn't want to hear that because God took my baby away. It made me angry at Him and everything else about Him.

After the funeral, it was clear that my daughter's death was tearing me apart. At that time all I could do was work and pray my way through it, but I couldn't get relief. Although many people tried to console me, my mother and Aunt Teresa assured me that God would give me the strength I needed.

Every day someone was reminding me that she was gone when they gave their condolences. I was tired of hearing, "I'm so sorry about your daughter."

If I Were God For One Day

By Dawn C. Mitchell (11 Years Old)

If I were God for one day (Which I will never be),
But if I were God for one day,
our world would be a beautiful world.

The air would not be polluted.

Everybody would have an all together different personality
Of course, I wouldn't take away their talents, but just make
them nicer people.

There would never be an energy crisis.

If I had a choice, I don't think I would like to be God, because
I don't think I'm reliable enough and I couldn't take the
responsibility of the world world

But just say I was God for just one day,
people would enjoy themselves.
All diseases would be cured
There'd be no such thing as "ugly" or "retarded" people

There'd be no unkind animals
All living things would be happy
No one would be sad for the rest of the day

I would just start the world over again
and make everybody and everything HAPPY.

Gail's Strength

Thank God I had my older daughter, Gail, she helped me get through it along with Bea and my band. Gail was also heartbroken by her sister's death. They were close and it was hard for her to lose Dawn. I didn't know she had been learning to play the bongo and conga drums until I walked in on her practicing one day. She blew me away!

Seeing that she needed a change, I took Gail on the road with me and the band when she was 18.
Traveling together during those dark days was a much needed source of joy and relief for the both of us. Healing after the loss of my daughter took a while. I dove deeper into my music and I began writing songs and performing more.

Back then, my walk with God wasn't as strong as it is now. I didn't think that my prayers meant anything, but I know now that God accepts the posture of our hearts. I prayed to God when my heart was heavy. Back then it didn't make sense to me how God was covering and taking care of me. God was using my family to lead me back to Him. I didn't understand what He was doing for me, but I do now. My pain has become my testimony.

This is a picture of Gail playing her drums.

Losing My Mother

A few years later, my mother began to suffer from arthritis. At first, I did not realize how ill she had become because she kept her ailments to herself. However, on what came to be her last visit to Pittsburgh in 1984, it almost seemed as if she was saying "good-bye." She was standing in my kitchen looking down at me at the other end of the counter. It seemed like she was watching me. I said, "Mom, [are] you okay?"

She said, "Oh yeah, I'm just looking at my baby." I didn't think anything else of it, but it did seem odd that she kept watching me during her trip. About a month after she returned to Buffalo, I received a call from my Aunt Mabel that my mother had been taken to the hospital. "Her arthritis caused a blood vessel to rupture," she told me. "Come see about her."

On the four hour drive from Pittsburgh to Buffalo I had time to think a lot. I saw a vision of a dark cloud looming over the hospital. It made me feel as if something was going wrong.

Upon reaching the hospital, I jumped out of the car and rushed into my mother's room. It shocked me that she was on life support. No one was in there but I called out to her, "Ma."

She couldn't talk because she was sedated and had a tube in her throat. I started to see white foam coming out of her mouth and I learned later that the tube had burst, which caused her death. I cried and I cried hard being in that room with my mother. I did not need to be strong for anyone else. I called out for help, "Nurse!" Everybody rushed in, and they asked me to step out of the room.

First, my daughter passed, then my mother – I was totally overcome with emotions. Being her only child, I had to plan my mother's funeral services. I had two of my friends help me with the music. One friend played and the other sang, "Precious Lord" at her funeral. Her pastor eulogized her at Calvary Baptist Church in Buffalo. It was a nice service because she was well loved. I was proud to send my mom home with excellence.

Aunt Teresa came from Chicago for the funeral. I was happy to see her, even under the circumstances. She said, "If you ever need to get away, come and spend time with me." I told her I would make plans to visit her that summer, but Aunt Teresa passed before I could make the visit. I was devastated.

Within a short period of time, I lost three people in my life that I loved dearly. I felt completely broken and devastated in my heart. At the time it seemed as if God was taking my loved ones away from me. I did not understand why they had to die. I felt like I was being punished for something I had done wrong. "Has God turned His back on me?" I asked myself.

I was hurting so much that when my uncle, Elwood Fields passed away in 1985, I could not go to his funeral. It was just too much death for me. I did not understand that God always knows what is best. I thought He was taking people away because I loved them more than Him. I had heard that God is a jealous God. I know now that everything was in His perfect plan for me.

"This certainly was not my plan; it was as if God was flipping the script and directing my path to important changes ahead."

~Pops

GOD FLIPPED THE SCRIPT

I fell in love with singing in Buffalo and after high school music grew into a business opportunity. I loved arranging, writing, producing, performing, and discovering new artists. Music was in my blood and I always knew there was much more to my musical career than singing on street corners. When our band started to become more recognized, we were given a lot more gig opportunities.

Around 1971 Bea and I decided to make Pittsburgh our home. It is centrally located within Pennsylvania and easy to get to Ohio, Virginia, New York, New Jersey and Maryland. We had a lot of shows in Harrisburg, Pennsylvania and Philadelphia, Pennsylvania, so it was an easy decision to make.

Bea and I rented an apartment when we first moved. The cost of living was different and we could not buy a house immediately. We kept our other home in Massillon for family and we were able to travel back and forth to Ohio to check on it with ease.

Moving to Pittsburgh

I loved the beauty of Pittsburgh and the lovingkindness and friendliness of the people. When we would sing, the audience expected nothing but the best from us. We didn't give them any junk; we gave them everything we had and they loved that about us.

I started picking up the local slang, saying things like "Yinz" which means "you all." I was already a football fan, but I became a Steelers fan like most of the people in the city. My favorite meal was from Birdie's Hurricane which was a club we used to play at regularly. I loved getting the big shrimp platters with fries; they were so good.

From singing at Birdies we met Gene Stevens who was a record producer at Pittsburgh International Records. He offered to record us in a studio in Ohio. We recorded a 45" record, "Don't Listen to Your Friends" written by Stanley Howard. In 1984, we recorded "I Can Feel Your Love Slippin' Away" and "Just Gonna Take My Time."

Things were going well for a while until disco and DJs started to make a come up. The entertainment scene was slowing down for live performances of bands and I needed to make money to take care of my family.

One Christmas Gene asked me if I was interested in working at his medical supply company that weekend to help him. I liked the work and ended up retiring from there after twenty years. The job allowed me to continue taking gigs on the weekend. Over time my work at the medical supply company began to overshadow our gigs. This certainly was not my plan; it was as if God was flipping the script and directing my path to important changes ahead.

"God expanded my territory and used me to do different things to encourage people with my music."

~Pops

WORKING FOR THE LORD

Sometime later, Bea and I started singing with God's Special Edition, a Pittsburgh gospel group under the direction of Lisa Brown. People in the group knew that we were Samson and Delilah. They did not feel that it was appropriate for us be in the gospel group with them because we sang "in the world." They were so holy that they could not see themselves. Some people wanted us to leave the group, but Lisa said we could stay.

That started our transition into gospel music in 1994. Pressure mounted from the group for me and Bea to find a church home and develop a relationship with God. Lisa invited us to visit with her at Mt. Ararat Baptist Church where she was an active member and choir director.

After a few visits at the church, the Holy Spirit led us to join. The message moved me and I started to cry before I went down to the altar with Bea. When I had joined church before it was because my mother had told me to. This time, God drew me to Him. We decided that we no longer wanted to play our music in night clubs. God had a way of working, it was a sudden stop, but a smooth transition for us.

Walking By Faith

Our hearts and minds had become completely devoted to gospel music. Even though I was not aware of what was going on then, I know now that this was part of God's plan for us and I have been at Mount Ararat for thirty years.

I joined the choir when I became a member of the church. Lisa trusted me to fill in for her on the organ if she ran late for service. Eventually playing led to a paid position with the church, thanks to my friend Valetta O'Kelly who advocated for me with the deacon board.

As I played for the chorus, I began worrying about how emotion filled I became when I played. I asked Lisa if I was a distraction and she in turn asked me "How do you feel?"

I told her, "When I played in the world I tried to please the people, and I gave them everything I had." In church I didn't like it when people watched me play because I didn't feel the same. I wanted to give God everything I had and it made me emotional because I didn't feel like I was doing enough for Him. It took time to learn how to move myself out of the way so that He could use me.

What I came to learn through Bible study, reading, and prayer was that ministry is about pleasing God. When you focus on pleasing God and giving Him the glory, the people will be blessed. I also learned as I grew in Christ, that people, from the pastor down, can let you down even when you try to do your best. Your best may never be good enough. People may not have your back, but God is always there-- providing what you need, when you need it.

Without God, no one gets blessed. In my performances I give my best. I rehearse with my group to make sure everything is correct. I can't just go up there and sing without rehearsing anything. Even when I was singing worldly music I had a high standard because I wanted the message to be valuable for my audience. They came to see us because they wanted to feel good and be satisfied by our performance when they went home.

Transition In Ministry

In 1995 our church had a split and several members left. I was not led to leave with the masses to go start a new congregation. When the fracture occurred, I knew God had other plans for me and I was relieved to be able to work in ministry differently. Most of my friends remained at Mount Ararat with me.

In 1997 Mount Ararat got a new pastor, which made a big difference in the church and in me. I felt myself growing more into the Word of God because of the anointing upon Rev. Dr. William H. Curtis. I liked him because he had a vision that inspired me to learn more about God. Not only did Pastor Curtis know the Word of God, but he also knew how to make the Word of God clear to me. Listening to my pastor, I understood God more.

Furthermore, despite preaching three sermons a weekend, Pastor Curtis always gave a different twist to everything he preached. There are many lessons I have learned sitting under my pastor and his teaching of the Word. One thing that I will always remember is that there is always room for growth in ministry. As I serve God I have come to understand that I must go through struggles because God has a plan and a purpose for my life.

This helped me understand what God was taking me through with losing my daughter, my mother and my aunt. God saw me through it all. I didn't know it at that moment in time. All I could say was going through those situations was, "Why me, poor me?" Now I know, that if I trust in the Lord and lean not to my own understanding, God will prepare and provide a way for me in life. He'll do the same for you (Proverbs 3:5-7).

With the vision of Pastor Curtis, the Mount Ararat choir hosted a live concert to record our first album, "Called to Relationship" in 2012. I was honored and blessed to write and lead the song, "You Can Count On It."

The Male Chorus

When the church split I became the director of Mt. Ararat's Male Chorus after Lisa changed her membership. Early on, I was blessed to make two great friends in ministry. They were Dwayne Fulton, Mount Ararat's Minister of Music, and Trini Massie, Mount Ararat's Minister of Worship. I learned so much from them.

I believe that God gave me the talent to minister in music. As a result of my service to God, I was led to do outreach in the community with the male chorus. I knew that there were people in the community who could not make it to church so I took church to them with the choir. We ministered at a senior citizen high rise, in nursing homes and in hospitals.

People love to see a bunch of men singing, but I teach the members of the male chorus that ministry is not just about getting up there on the platform to sing songs. I tell them, "We have to know what we are singing about." When we sing we make a joyful noise unto the Lord. The main thing is not just learning a song to sing, but living a life that's worth singing about.

I lead by example. I have heard all my life, "A man shouldn't cry, or be emotional." When it comes to serving God there is no limitation. We cry because we give God everything we have; this is not for show and tell. We take our ministry seriously because we know that we are alive by His grace. We are witnesses for the Lord.

I used to think that I could only get a thrill from being with a woman, but God fulfills my every need. As my faith has grown with the Lord, I get overjoyed by His presence. This is what I want the male chorus to know and the example I want them to have about walking with Christ.

I wrote a prayer for the Male Chorus. We always pray it together before we minister anywhere:

"*Lord,*

Please use me as your instrument to touch other's lives. Help me not to be concerned about what title I hold, but instead, my life may show others your grace.

God's gift to us is not for us only but to share with others.

Amen."

From Samson to Pops

I was given the name "My Poppa Bear" by my spiritual daughter, Latika. Another spiritual daughter, Kimi, called me "Poppy." The name "Pops" is a derivative of both names so I changed my stage name from Samson to my ministry name, Anthony "Pops" Mitchell. God flipped the script and allowed me to make another transition.

When I changed my name people asked me, "How can you do that?" They expected me to feel ashamed about the fact that I used to be Samson of Samson and Delilah. The funny thing is, Samson is a Biblical name, you can see where I came from. God was working even through that time in my life. I didn't have anything to do with it, God has a way of working us for what He wants. Work through those things and God will get you to where you want to be in life.

I do everything I do as unto the Lord (Colossians 3:23-24). Daily, my love for God grows more and more. I am an example of God's mercy and serving the Lord as a new creation, not the man I used to be. I keep serving Him after all of these years because of my love for Him and the appreciation for the gifts He has given me to serve Him. I am grateful that God has brought me through, He knows my future.

God expanded my territory and used me to do different things to encourage people with my music. I prayed and God made a way for me to record my first gospel album, "Lord Because Of My Faith in You" because I know that I am who I am today only because of God's grace, mercy, and love for me. I recorded the album in 2012 in Pittsburgh, Pennsylvania. My wife, Bea, and several close friends joined me on the record.

Spreading The Ministry To Youth

I minister to other people because I want to let them know that God brought me through. I don't test-i-LIE about what God has done, I testify of His goodness. Over the years I have been able to work with groups to help young people. Bea and I have worked together to support several youth groups including the Miss Black Teenage Pageant.

In 1992, Bea and I collaborated with Pittsburgh Job Corps as their choir directors. Some of the young people couldn't afford to go to college and went to learn trades at Job Corps. It made me feel happy that they were so thankful to work with us. We wrote and produced a song called "Pittsburgh Job Corps" which spread a positive message about everybody being able to become somebody.

Mel Blount, a former player for the Pittsburgh Steelers is a good friend of mine from Mount Ararat. He founded a youth home for troubled boys in Claysville, PA. After service one Sunday, Mel approached me and asked me and Bea, "Would you come be the choir directors at the Mel Blount Youth Home?"

Bea and I both were excited for the opportunity and I said, "Yeah, we'll do it." I wanted to do anything to support the young men in their pursuit of living a better life. Bea and I invited a couple of friends, Penny Turner and Stevie Akers to join us in working with the youth. We started the group "Pops and Friends" and every weekend we traveled about 45 minutes to teach gospel songs to the young men. We sang mostly Kirk Franklin songs because that is what they liked. The group was invited to sing at various programs and churches in and around Pittsburgh.

Working with the Mel Blount Youth Home and Pittsburgh Job Corps changed me because it gave me an opportunity to encourage children to see that they can make a better life for themselves. God confirmed for me through that work that He has equipped me to do a special work for Him. These opportunities came to me, I wasn't out there looking for them, but God saw fit to use me and for that, I am grateful.

"God opened a door for me."

~Pops

A NEW MINISTRY FAMILY

During COVID-19 in 2020-2021, I was introduced to a small, local church, called United Vision. Life was hard for everybody and musicians stopped getting paid. There was no way to make money and I couldn't go anywhere or do anything; God opened a door for me. A lady kept calling me and asking, "Can you play for me one Sunday?" She said, "I've been trying to get you for the longest."

Serving Through COVID-19

I decided to visit United Vision and I played for them one Sunday. The pastor asked me to come back the next Sunday. Because I wasn't playing with the band and the male chorus wasn't singing, I kept going back to the church until eventually, I became their minister of music.

The members are good hearted people and they loved me. I haven't seen anything like the way they treat me and Bea, they never leave her out. Some of them call her "Little Mama."

When I started working for the church, they paid me for a whole month ahead of time. Sometimes at rehearsals on Thursdays they buy food for me and my wife to take home, and on holidays they bless us too. I mean, they are just the nicest people. Being with them feels like being with my family in Memphis.

Along with four ladies, we formed a group "Pops and the Sisters" to provide United Vision's music ministry on Sundays. This union is another example of how God surrounds me with love. After COVID when I went back to working with the Male Chorus at Mount Ararat they said, "Do what you have to do over at Mount Ararat, as long as you give us what we need, that's alright."

I love serving God at Mount Ararat and United Vision.

*"I know there is a God.
I have seen His amazing work in
my life."*

~Pops

A BLESSED MAN

I'm not the richest man in the world, but I am rich in love. I am rich because He's always providing me with what I need. And today I'm so happy. I've got a home and a lovely wife. I've got all the things that I need. Some people have all the money in the world, but they don't have what I have.

I'm grateful for how God has worked in my life. He will do the same for you if you let Him. Let God have His way in your life and things will work out fine. I learned that I can depend on Him and I count on Him for anything. I just have to wait, listen, and be patient. He's done a lot in my life.

I didn't make hit records like I wanted to make and I have had some messed up record deals. What got me through it was following people's love wherever I went. I show appreciation because when God flipped the script, nothing decreased it increased, because of the love we have for each other.

I am continuing to grow in my spiritual walk with God and in my music ministry. I have joy in my life because I have a purpose and a reason to be. God does so much for me, I can't even thank Him enough, but I can write songs and words of praise and worship to Him and I'm glad about that. It's good to be at this point in my life.

It's not going to easy for anybody young. They are going to have to go through to get through and they need our help to get to all those things. We all have to go through changes. I have heard people complain that secular artists are "working for the devil." I don't agree with that. God has a plan for all of us. I am not ashamed of where I started out.

God had a plan and a purpose for my life, and I realize that now. Wherever you start out, eventually God is going to get His way.

My songwriting is how I share my expressions to God. I give my thanks to Him for all that He's given me for without God, none of this would be possible; He has proven Himself time and time again. I think back to times when I stood up to sing and with no voice and God restored it in ministry. It humbles me that God has used me to bless other people.

I don't always talk about the things that God has brought me through. Sometimes when I am ministering I feel pain in my back. Other times it is hard for me to walk around, but when I'm doing ministry, I'm fine, feeling joy. God is my support system when I am performing, doing ministry, or serving at funerals. When ministry is over, I go sit down and it's time to rest.

Sometimes when I am singing I begin to cry and worship God. I just tell Him how much I love Him and how thankful I am for all of the things that He has done for me. If you see me in ministry sometimes I can barely get through ag song without crying.

It's crazy to me when I hear people say, "There is no God." I know there is a God. I have seen His amazing work in my life. It's just so, so powerful to know that I'm loved and that He works His way through me to help others.

"You will get through because of the grace of God."

~Pops

GO THROUGH TO GET THROUGH

As I look back over my life, I realize God was always redirecting me to His purpose and plan.

When I made plans and pursued projects that were difficult, did not work out, or got rejected, God was always behind the scenes working on my behalf. I learned how to let pain mature me; it provided a path for deepening my relationship with Him. My disappointments turned into blessings and all things have worked together in God's timing.

Advice for Musicians

I have been in the music industry for almost 70 years and I have advice for a young person starting out. On my birthday in 2024, I will turn 82, I knew a few things that can help you. As I look back, I want to share some things I wish I would have known when I was younger. It will be a growing process to get to know God. When you study His Word, go to Bible classes, and get with people who know Him, that can lead you on the right trail.

The way the world is today, there is not enough love. For me being fatherless, fortunately I had people around me who loved me and carried me through things that were hurtful in my life. My mother and father came into my life when God appointed the right season. Through it all, He was with me.

1. Keep God First

God had to work out salvation in my life. When I was born again, He had a plan for what He wanted me to do. My name kept changing as I grew in him. It changed to "Samson and Delilah" and spiritually to "Pops." God has used me to tell people in the club that they can be changed like I was. It did bother me when people would make comments about me having "worked for the devil" in my past. Older people especially used to say, "Stop singing that devil music." It put out a fear in my heart about what I could do and what I shouldn't do.

I had to come to the realization that keeping God first helped me to grow into everything that I am. All of my gifts come from God. I wasn't working for the devil because I was taking stuff that God gave me and using it for Him. When I did sing secular songs I liked clean, nice songs about love, you know? My reputation wasn't known for being nasty on stage.

God will take you through some things to get you to where He wants you to be. Even back then, our group signed fake contracts and people used us. It took faith and heart to keep going even when I was disgusted by the negative circumstances. People will make you promises and they will let you down, but God always keeps His word. A lot of things happened to me that made me want to give up everything, but I had the determination to continue.

2. Be A Pillar

Be a pillar for kids to lean on. When you know the Lord you can lead them in the right direction. You can't always just tell a kid about things; they have to see it in you. Be an example, not just someone who says, "Do as I say and not as I do." You don't want the children to wonder about your faith and how you live your life for Christ.

As you recognize that God is in control of everything in your life, you will be more focused when you experience troubles. When you recite scriptures such as, "I can do all things through Christ," you know that He will never forsake you and you stand in confidence that God will strengthen you. Let people see God in your life. You never want anyone to say, "Why are you telling me about Christ when he ain't done nothing for you?" Show them God through your walk.

3. Do Not Rush The Process

If you love to sing or love to play, love it. Give your best of it. The Lord will lead you in the direction, along with your parents or a mentor who follows

Christ. Stay connected to people who are truthful with you and want to see you succeed. Try not to allow people to bash you or force you into anything you don't feel comfortable doing.

Be prayerful that you run into the right people. You may encounter people who will take advantage of you and skimp out on your payments, but don't quit the music. Learn the lessons and keep going.

Sometimes I ran into the upright people in my life, and sometimes I didn't. It's like Scripture said, God can use anybody to get His work done. God can use anybody to give you a message of what He intends for you.

You're gonna make mistakes. God is working out things when you can't see it. He is so perfect that He knows every strand of hair on your head. We all have to walk by faith and not by sight. You have to grow to learn the words you study in the Bible; let it be embedded in your heart.

4. *Know the Difference Between Right and Wrong*

Growing up, I was taught the difference between what's right and what's wrong. If you don't have a mother or father, you are still accountable to learn what's worthy to do and what's wrong to do, that is what people call "common sense." You may do a lot of crazy things because you are mad or angry about your family situation. Find a way to break out of that negative mindset.

5. Love Your Music

Through hurt, pain, heartaches, ups and downs and people letting you down, you've got to really love what you're doing. Be determined to reach your goal. Some days you're going to be happy running from one place to the other and other days, you'll feel like you're sliding downhill.

When I sang in the secular world I loved to sing love songs to display what I wanted out of love. When I performed I had to perform it coming from me as if I was going through something. Through falling in and out of love I wrote songs to really have a meaning to them. It was almost like I was acting in a play— showing what each character needed to survive.

God gave you the gift of music. When you feel down, He will lead you and guide you to do things you ordinarily wouldn't be able to do. Give your gift back to God and watch Him use you.

6. Go Through To Get Through

You can't feel like you're gonna be perfect; you're gonna make mistakes. Christ said we were born imperfect but God has a way of working out things when you can't see because He is perfect. He knows everything about you. He knows all about you, even every hair on your head.

You can't see it. You can't feel it. You don't understand it sometimes. But you've got to have faith to believe that He will make a way out of no way. Scriptures like Philippians 4:19, "My God will supply all my needs," those are not words you just say, those are words you have to learn to believe. When you go through your trial you can recite Philippians 4:13 which says, "I can do all things through Christ who gives me strength." You've got to know that you know that you know.

You may ask yourself, "Why am I going through this?" You may get down on yourself when you see others achieving things that you haven't accomplished yet. Don't say, "Poor me."

We are all created differently, and everything's gonna happen with everybody differently, for the good and bad. Some people you see that look like they are making it have problems too, life happens. They may not be as happy as you think they are for different reasons. They may not have God in their life or they may have other people helping them look good. You don't know if they are getting the finances and other things that they really need.

Final Reflections

I have learned that in today's world you gotta go through to get through. What that means is the hurt, pain, and suffering is necessary for you to get where God wants you to be. Sometimes God allows things to happen to get you where He wants you to be and you can't change that.

God made it so easy that we think it's hard. Walk by faith not by sight. That will help you embed the words you study in the Bible in your heart. That's why we sing the song that says, "You are my strength..."

You have to trust in the Lord for everything these days; if you don't have trust, it can be rough for you. Trust in God never stops, it grows every day. The more you love Him, you understand what He does. One day you will say, "My goodness, I thank God, I couldn't do none of this stuff on my own." You will get through because of the grace of God. He is not through with you yet.

MUSIC BIBLIOGRAPHY

Secular Songs

Baby, I Need Your Good Lovin'
Don't Listen to Your Friends
Slippin' Away
Will You Be Ready?
Love Has So Many Changes
There's a D.J. in Your Town
Time To Prove My Love To You
Just Gonna Take My Time

Gospel Songs

There Is A Name Above Every Name
Confess With Your Mouth
It's So Good To Say Thank You
He's Number One
It Ain't About You
Keep on Praying
God Will Make A Way
I Am Depending On Jesus
I Will Praise Thee
For Your Word
Holy Spirit Fall On Me
Send Your Spirit For My Break Through
I Need You Lord
If I Let God Have His Way
Lord Because of My Faith In You

SOME OF MY FAVORITE BOOKS

- Dunnett, Walter M. *Revelation: God's Final Words to Man*
- Groeschel, Craig. *It: How Churches and Leaders can Get it and Keep It*
- Lea Jr., Claybon. *Giant Lessons From David: Managing The Journey of Success*
- Ortbert, John. *When The Game Is Over It All Goes Back In The Box.*
- Stein. Robert H. *Playing By The Rules: A Basic Guide to Interpreting The Bible*
- Weah, Lisa. *Leading With a Left Hand*
- Young. William P. *The Shack*

Books by My Pastor *Rev. Dr. William H. Curtis*

- *Dressed for Victory: Putting on the Full Armour of God*
- *Faith: Learning To Live Without Fear*

ABOUT THE AUTHOR

 Anthony Mitchell has always lived a life of music. He developed his love for music at an early age, teaching himself how to play the organ, singing on corners in New York with friends and using his vocals as a lead singer and in the background. He writes, produces and arranges.

Born in Memphis, Tennessee, with ties to Chicago and New York, Anthony is affectionately known to those who love him as "Pops" or "Papa Tony."

As a producer, songwriter, organist, arranger, lead and backup singer, music is his ministry. He has been blessed to work with Dionne Warwick, The O'Jay's, Stevie Wonder, The Isley Brothers and many other well-known artists.

Pops lives in Pittsburgh, Pennsylvania with his wife, Bea and attends Mount Ararat Baptist Church under the leadership of Rev. Dr. William H. Curtis. At Mount Ararat Pops is the director and spiritual leader for the Male Chorus. He released an album in 2012 entitled, "Lord, Because of My Faith in You" *My Life and Walk with God* is Pop's autobiography and first book.

"I now understand that I had to go through it to get through it."

~Pops